The Triads of Ireland

An Illustrated Collection

Olivia Wylie

For those who take the time to listen.

Introduction

Three candles that illumine every darkness:
Truth
Nature
Knowledge

Those words were inscribed upon the vellum page of the Book of Húi Maine some time in 1391. Perhaps the man who wrote it did so while looking at his own beeswax candle while the freezing sleet of an Irish winter beat on the stone walls around him. His life was like nothing we know today, and yet the words he wrote then still ring true.
The passage above is part of a vibrant and uniquely Irish poetic form: Triads. Resembling haikus to the modern Western eye, the Triad follows the formula of setting a concept for discussion in the first line and describing its salient qualities in the next three lines. The triads are often deeply evocative, as in this example:

Moaighthe:
médaighthe, sochair, do neoch.

Three sounds of increase:
the lowing of a cow in milk,
the din of a smithy,
the swish of a plough.

But the form just as easily turns itself to humor, and in some examples you can almost hear the sly smile in the tone of the writer as they pen:

An-onoruighther nó uaislighther:
pluice ag síneadh a beoil.
righe a bhronn
righe a bhuilg

Three things that constitute a fool:
blowing out his cheek,

blowing out his satchel,
blowing out his belly.

We are lucky enough to enjoy these writings through the work of Kuno Meyer, a scholar who fought his way through the crumbling manuscripts of the Book of Ballymote, the Book of Húi Maine, the Yellow Book of Lecan and other faded vellum manuscripts with their cramped writing spelling out Old Irish words. From these sources he collated and wrote 'The Triads Of Ireland', collecting as many triads as it was possible to find in 1906. It was originally published as volume 13 of the Todd Lecture Series of the Royal Irish Academy. The publisher was Hodges, Figgis, & Co., Ltd. of Dublin and London. This seminal translation is the source for most modern studies on the topic.

In this book I have illustrated the triads that still hold lessons for us today. Take a moment. Turn the page. Let yourself be lost in the words.

Life

Triads on Good Land and Good Living

Three drops of

life:

    a drop of

    blood,

        a tear-drop,

            a drop of

            sweat

Three slender things
that best support the
world:

the slender stream of

milk that feeds the

calf,

the slender blade of

green corn upon the

ground,

the slender thread in the hand

of a skilled woman

Three things that
show every good
man:
his skill in a
trade,
his
valour,
his
piety

Three hands
that are best
in the world:

the hand of

a good

carpenter,

the hand

of a skilled

woman,

the hand

of a good

smith

Three
things that make
a welcome:
An open smile,
a full cauldron,
a warm fire

Three
preparations of
a good man's
house:
the ale-cup,
the bath, the hearth

Three
maidens
that bring love
to good fortune:
silence, diligence, sincerity.

Three glories of a gathering:
a beautiful wife, a good horse, a swift
hound

Two brothers:

prosperity and husbandry

Three things that mark the fortunate folk:
steadiness,
modesty,
sobriety

Three
deaths
that are better
than life:

the death of a bright

salmon,

the death of a fat pig,
the death of a
caught thief

Three deaths
that promise
life:

a deer
shedding
horns,

a wood
shedding
leaves,
cattle
shedding their
coats

Three excellent things for a
householder:
proposing to a good
woman, serving
a good chief,
exchanging
for good
land

Three sparks that
kindle love: a fair
face, fair demeanour,
fair speech

Three sounds of increase:
the lowing of a cow in milk,
the din of a smithy,
the swish of a plow

Three renovators of

the world:

the womb of a

woman,

the udder of

a cow,

the anvil of

a smith

Three welcomes
of an alehouse:
plenty,
kindliness
and
art

Three keys that
unlock thoughts:
drunkenness,
trustfulness,
love

Three shouts of
a good warrior's
house:
the shout of
gift-giving,
the shout of
sitting down,
the shout of
rising up

Three things
for which an

enemy is

loved:

wealth,

beauty,

worth

Three
burdens
that are
better
than joy: the
weight of pigs fed
upon acorns,
the heaviness
of a ripe field,
the burden of a wood
groaning with fruit

Three fewnesses that are better than plenty:

a fewness of fine words,

a fewness of cows on grass,

a

fewness

of friends

around ale

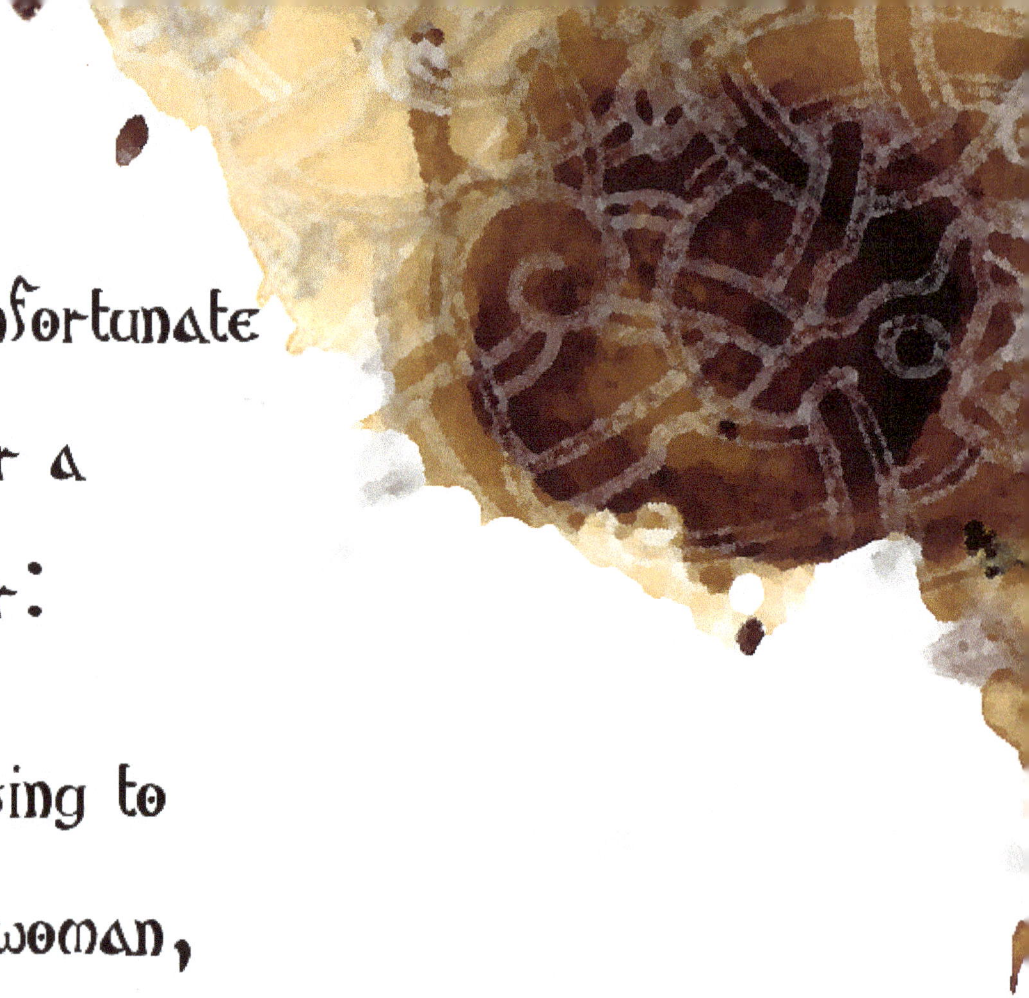

Three unfortunate
things for a
householder:

proposing to
a bad woman,
serving a bad
chief, exchanging for
bad land

Three things
that show
a
weak
man:
bitterness,
hatred,
cowardice

Three
rejoicings
that are worse
than sorrow:
the joy of a man who
has defrauded another,
the joy of
a man telling
lies,
the joy
of a man
who has shed
his father's blood

Three things
for which
a friend
is hated:

trespassing,

a distant

manner,

fecklessness

The three chief sins:

avarice,

    gluttony,

  lust

Three laughing-stocks
of the world:

an angry man,

a jealous man,

a miser

Three rude ones of
the world: a youngster
mocking an old man,
a healthy person
mocking an invalid,
a wise man
mocking
a fool

Three things that constitute
a buffoon:
blowing out his cheek,
blowing out his satchel,
blowing out his belly

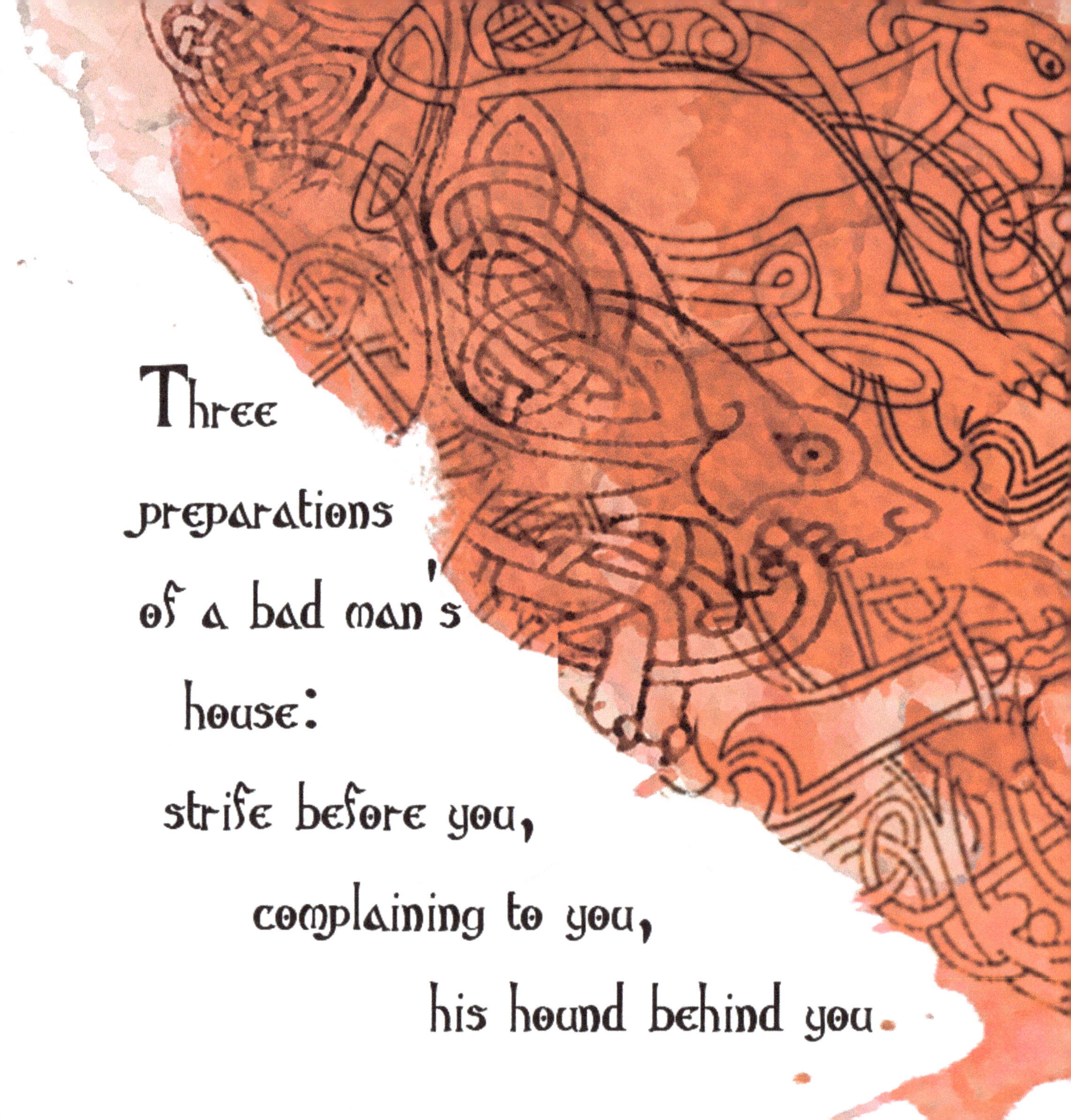
Three
preparations
of a bad man's
house:
strife before you,
complaining to you,
his hound behind you.

Three sons whom
folly bears to anger:
frowning, arguing,
mockery

Three

rejoicings

followed by sorrow:

a carouser's,

a thief's,

a gossip's

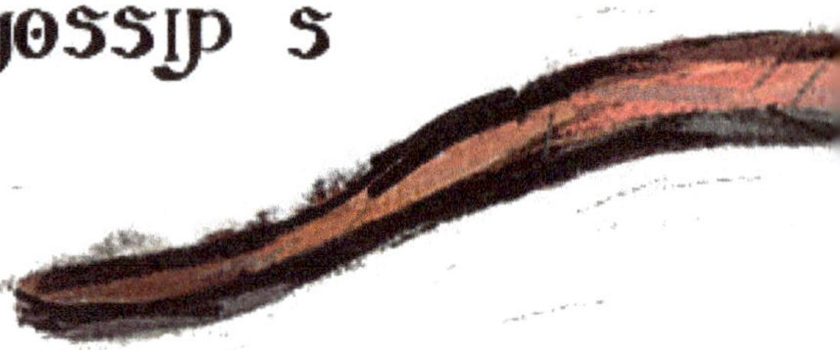

Three maidens that
bring hatred upon
misfortune: chatter,
laziness,
insincerity

Three ungentlemanly things:

the interrupting of
stories,
the making of mischief,
words that raise a blush

Four elements of folly:
silliness, bias, wrangling,
foulmouthedness

Three whose spirits are highest:

the student who completes
their studies,
the boy who puts away
his childhood clothes,

the
maiden
who becomes
a woman

Learning

Triads On Wisdom And Skill

Three candles that

illumine every

darkness:

truth,
nature,
knowledge

Three signs of wisdom:
patience, closeness,
precience

Three nurses of dignity:

a good mind,

a good memory,

a good soul

Three ornaments of wisdom:
an abundance of knowledge,
a number of precedents,
a good counsel

Three well-bred sisters:
constancy, well-spokenness,
kindliness

Three ruins of wisdom:

ignorance,

inaccurate knowledge,

forgetfulness

Three ill-bred sisters:
shiftlessness, grudging,
closefistedness

Three things
that constitute
a carpenter:
a mind for the wood,
a hand for the compass,
an arm for the stroke
of the axe

Three things

that constitute a physician:

a complete cure, a healing

without blemish, a painless

examination

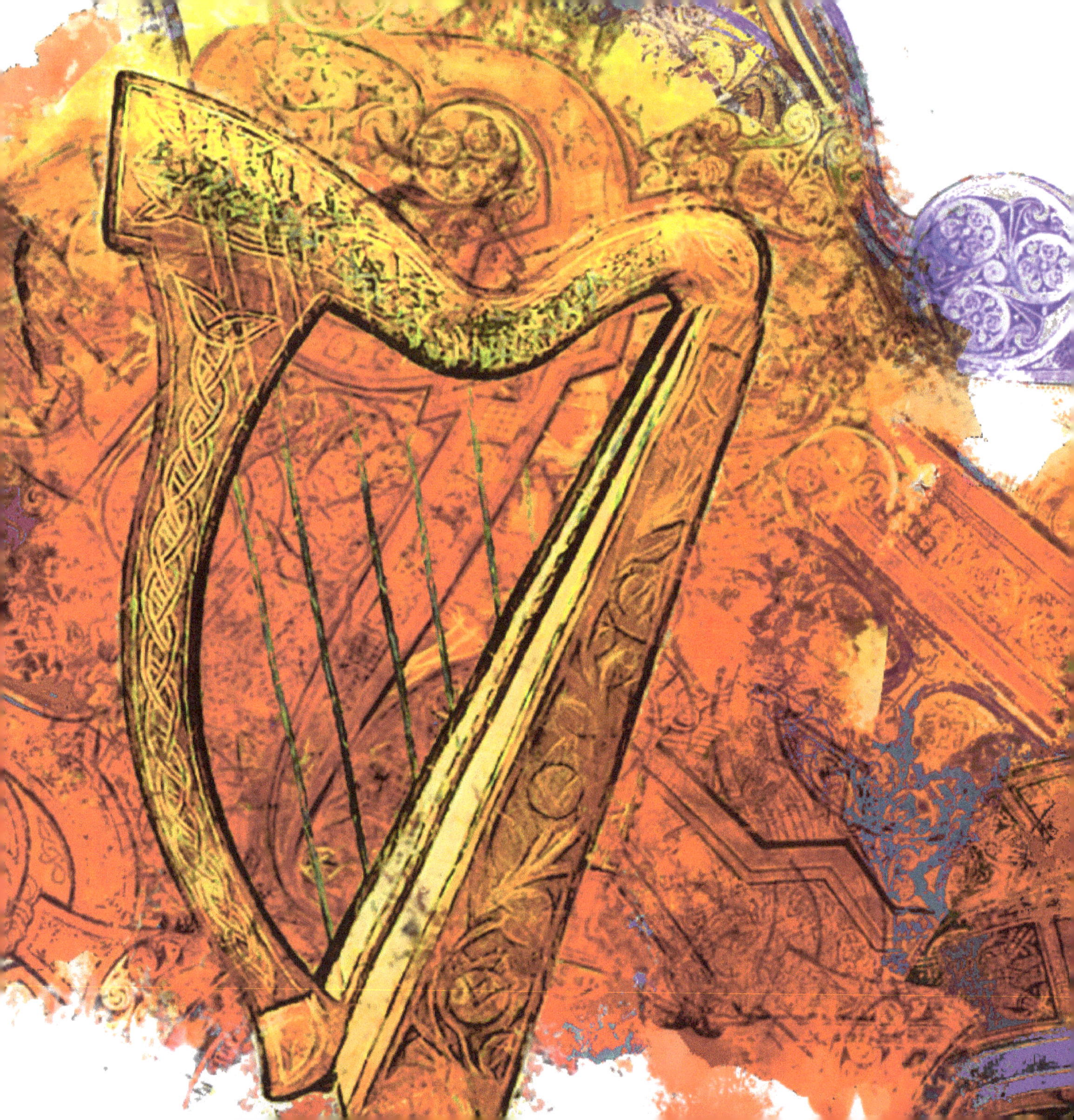

Three things that constitute a harper:

a tune

to make you cry,

a tune to make you laugh,

a tune

to let you

sleep

Three things that constitute a poet:
a knowledge that illumines,
a mind for memory,
a tongue for
improvisation

Three glories of speech:
steadiness,
wisdom,
brevity

Three
hateful things in speech:
stiffness,
obscurity,
a bad delivery

Three who do not adjudicate,
though they may have wisdom:
a man who sues,
a man who is being sued,
a man who is bribed to give
judgment.

Three doors
of falsehood:

an angry pleading,

a shifting foundation
of knowledge,

giving information without memory

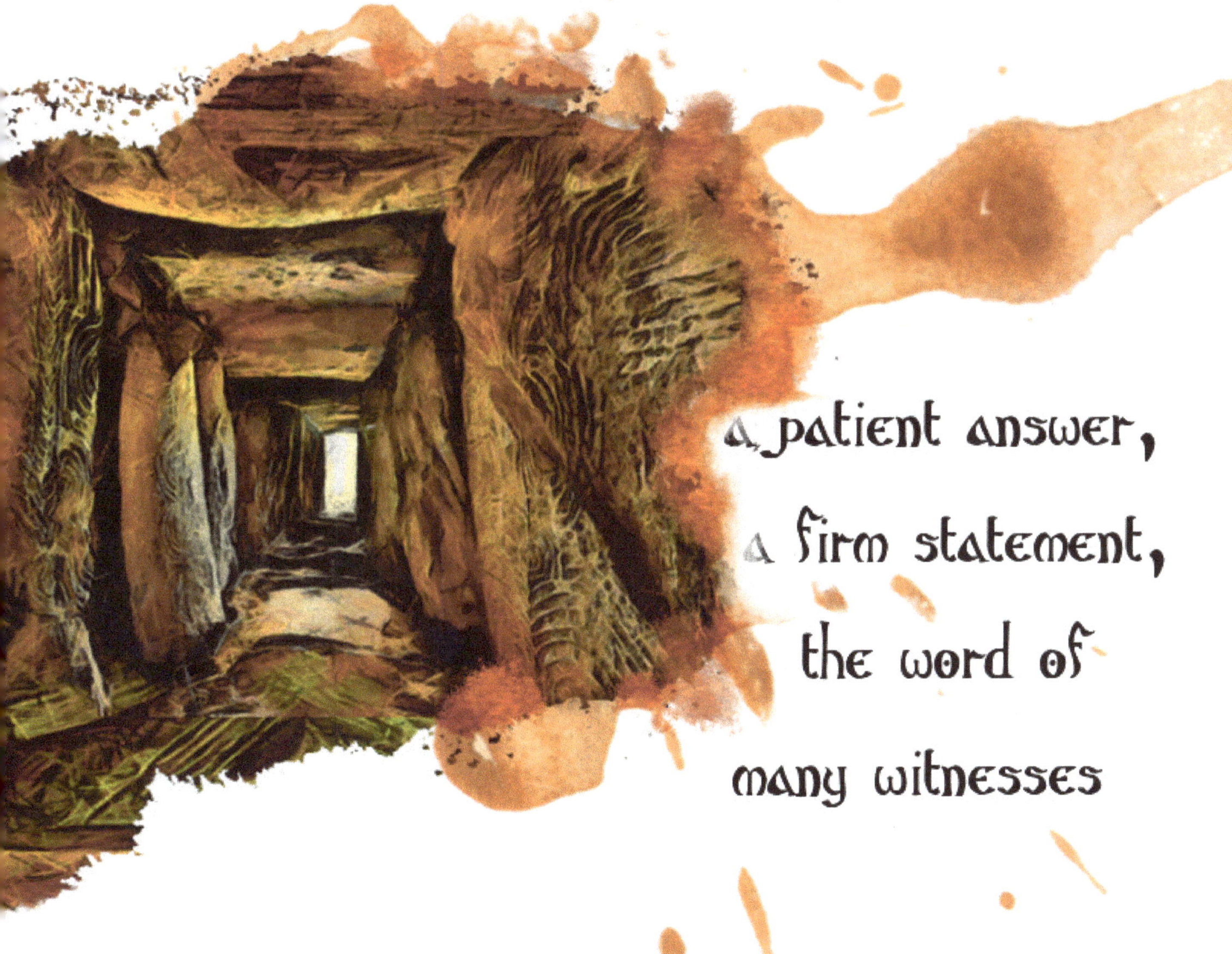
Three doors through which truth is seen:

a patient answer,

a firm statement,

the word of

many witnesses

Three things
that make a fool wise:
learning, steadiness, listening

Three things
that make a wise man foolish:
quarreling, anger, drunkenness

Three speeches that
are better than
silence:
the speaking of
courageous words,
the spreading of
knowledge,
praise
given to skill

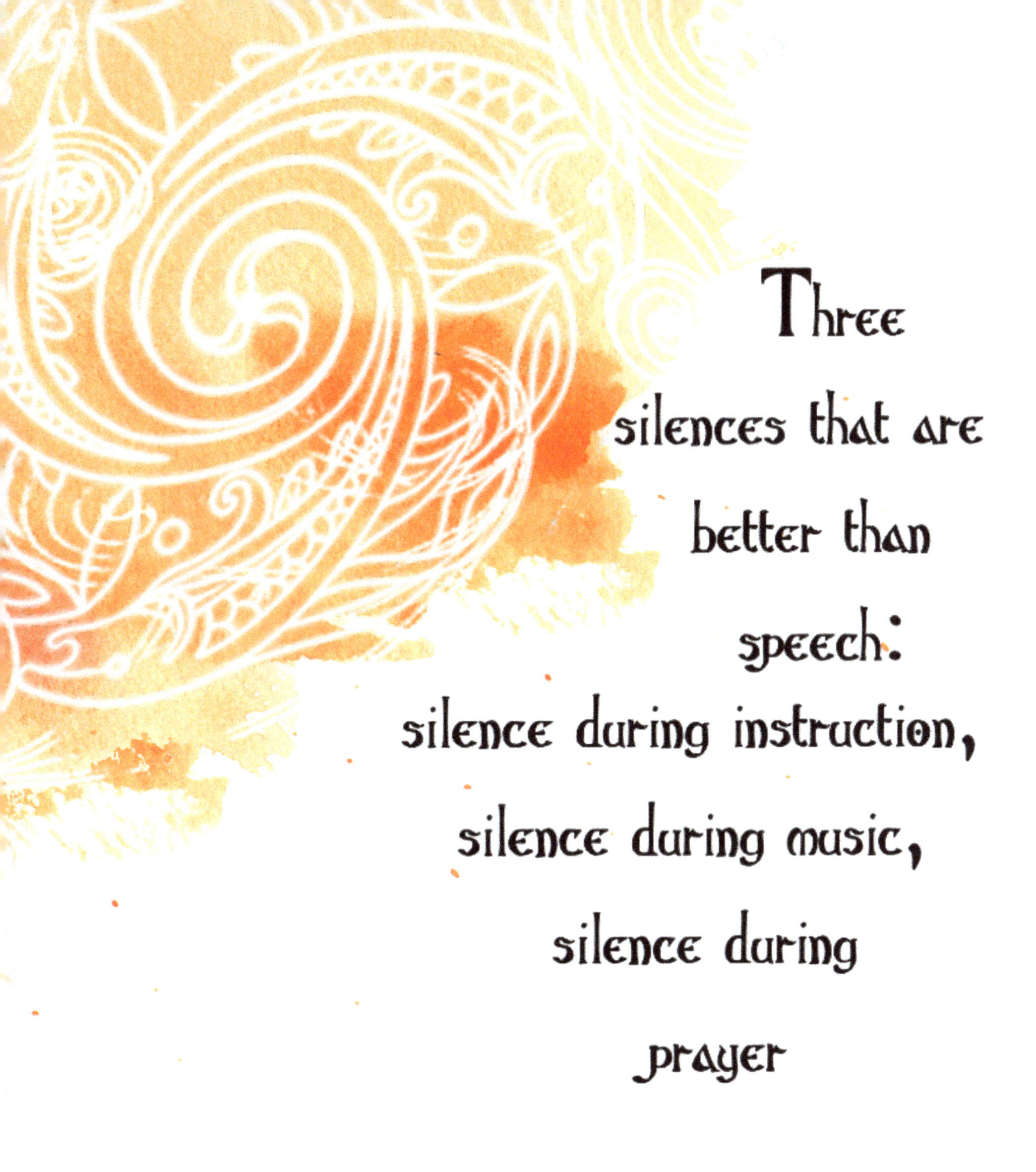

Three
silences that are
better than
speech:
silence during instruction,
silence during music,
silence during
prayer

Three signs
of folly:

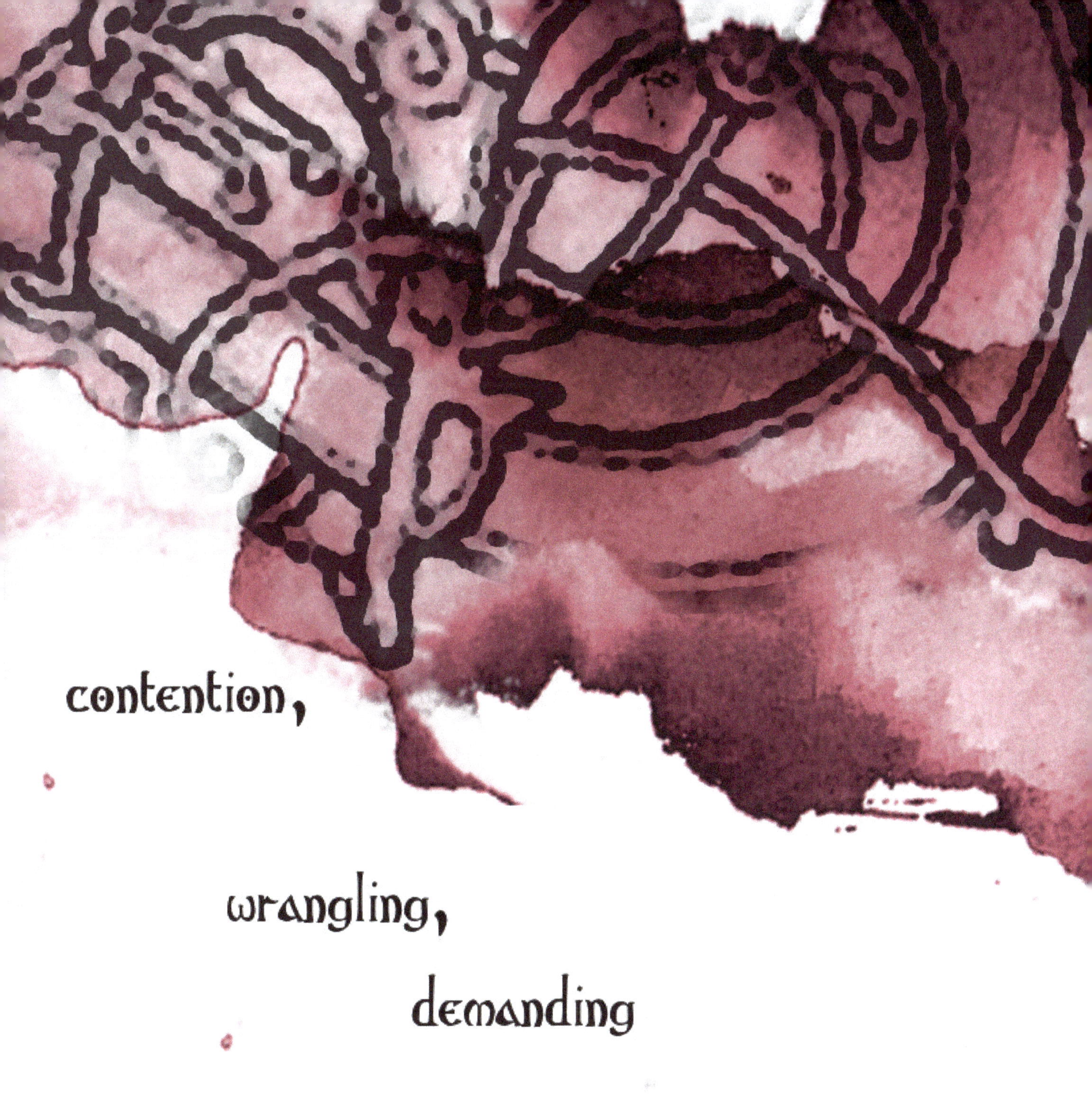

contention,
wrangling,
demanding

Four elements of wisdom:

patience, quiet,

sobriety,

well-spokenness

for the patient person is wise,
the quiet person is a sage,
the sober person is reasoning,
and the well-spoken person is
well-mannered

Leadership

Triads On The Art Of Statecraft

Three rocks to which lawful
behaviour is tied:

the community,
the chieftain,
the family

Three things
that constitute
a king:

the binding of contracts,
the feeding of the folk,
the health of the land

Three things
that are best for a chief:

justice,

peace,

an army

Three things
that are worst for a chief:

sloth,
treachery,
evil counsel

Three things that
characterise a patient person:
still hands, a quiet mouth,
listening ears

Three chains
by which evil propensity is bound:
the given word, the given rule,
the good law

Four bosom friends
of a chief:

a poet with satire and praise,

a chronicler of good memory

with narration and story-telling,

a judge with wise counsel,

a historian with ancient lore

Four scorned foes

of a chief:

a foolish man, a slavish man,

a lying man, a man

who has nothing

worth hearing

to say

Three sons whom discipline

bears to wisdom:

valour, generosity,

laughter

Three ruins of a tribe:

a lying chief,

a false judge,

a lustful priest

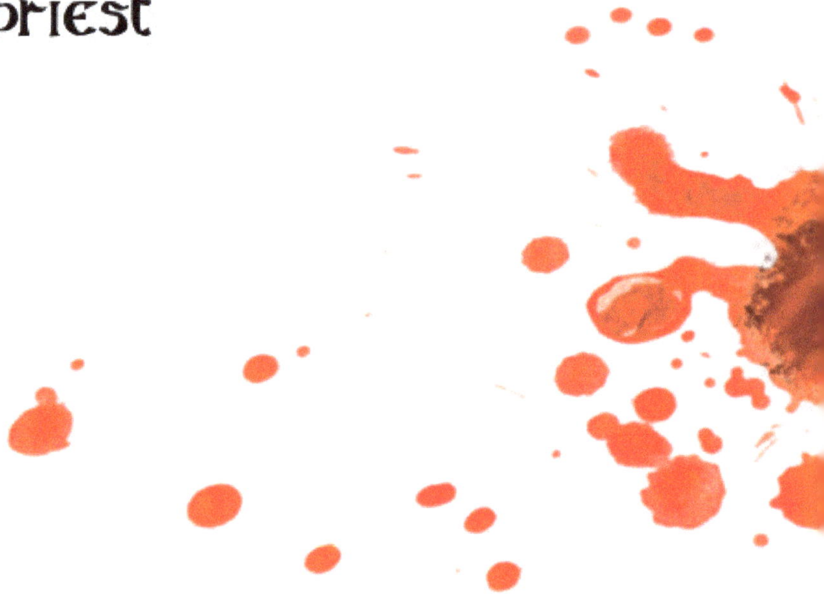

Three

lasting things in the world:

Grass, bronze,

yew wood

That is all

Original Irish For the Triads Included In This Book, Art Style and Featured Artifacts

I've allowed myself a little artistic license with a few of the triads in these illustrations, to allow them to flow more naturally for modern readers. In this appendix I've given the original Irish and the exact translations from Kuno Meyer's work for each piece, to keep us all honest. Please note that, when Meyer was not sure of a letter, he replaced it with a number in his work. If numbers appear in odd places below, this is the reason.

 I'd also like to add a note giving name and credit to the beautiful artifacts that I've drawn inspiration from to create this book. Despite the appearance, the illustrations in this volume are actually a form of digital art. To create these pieces, I took several steps. After considering each triad and its cultural connotations, I looked through stock images I've collected over time, showing many of the treasures of the Celtic world and illustrations from a number of illuminated manuscripts. I usually choose specific pieces for their appearance, their cultural meanings, or their colors in order to use as a reference piece. I then created digital paintings based on these artifacts and natural parts of the ancient Celtic world, overlaying them with celtic knotwork based on manuscripts contemporary to the period in which the Brehons were memorizing Triads as part of their training.

Below are a list of the named artifacts used as inspiration and reference.

*Note: When unsure of a letter in his work transcribing from the crumbling manuscripts, Meyer used numbers as a placeholder. I will continue his convention.

Illustration 1

Triad 126:

Trí bainne cétmuintire:
bainne fola, bainne dér, bainne aillse

Three drops of a wedded woman: a drop of blood, a tear-drop, a drop of sweat.

Art Based On: Triad carvings, Newgrange, Co. Meath, Ireland

Illustration 2

Triad 75:

Trí cóil ata ferr:
folongat in mbith:
cóil srithide hi folldeirb,
cóil foichne for tuinn, cóil snáithe dar dorn
dagmná.

Three slender things that best support the world: the slender stream of milk from the cow's dug into the pail, the slender blade of green corn upon the ground, the slender thread over the hand of a skilled woman.

Art Based On: Carving of St. Bridget milking a cow, west face of St. Michael's tower, Glastonbury Tor, UK.

Illustration 3

Triad 196:

Tréde faillsiges cach ndagfheras: dán, gaisced, crésine.

Three things that show every good man: a special gift,* valour, piety.

Trí duirn ata dech for bith: dorn degsháir, dorn degmná, dorn deggobann.

Three hands that are best in the world: the hand of a good carpenter, the hand of a skilled woman, the hand of a good smith.

Art Based On: Anvil excavated in Co. Louth, courtesy of Irish Agricultural Museum Co. Wexford, Ireland. Brooch from the Ardagh Hoard, courtesy of National Museum of Ireland, Dublin. Knotwork, *Book of Kells*.

Illustration 4

Triad 97

Trí fuiric thige degduni: cuirm, fothrucud, tene mór.

Three preparations of a good man's house: ale, a bath, a large fire.

Irish for the triad on welcome no longer exists. Recorded in footnote of the Triads of Ireland by Kuno Meyer, volume 13 of the Todd Lecture Series, Royal Irish Academy

Art Based On: Illustration from the Book of Kells, knotwork from the *Book of the Dun Cow.*

Illustration 5

Triad 110

Trí hingena berta seirc do cháintocud: túa, éscuss, idnae.

Three maidens that bring love to good fortune: silence, diligence, sincerity.

Triad 88

Trí búada téiti:
ben cháem, ech maith, cú lúath.

Three glories of a gathering:
a beautiful wife, a good horse, a swift hound.

Art Based On: Comb made of bone from Langbank Crannog,
Renfrewshire, AD 1-200.

Gold lunula and disks, Museum of Ireland. Dating range of
2460–2040 BC.

Illustration 6

Triad 134

Dá derbráthair:
tocad 7 brugaide.

Two brothers:
prosperity and husbandry.

Triad 187

Trí túarascbaid cach ngenmnaide:
fosta, féile, sobraide.

Three things that characterise every
chaste person: steadiness, modesty,
sobriety.

Art Based On: Sickle, courtesy of Irish Agricultural Museum Co.
Wexford, Ireland.

Illustration 7

Triad 92

Trí báis ata ferr bethaid:
bás iach, bás muicce méithe, bás foglada.

Three deaths that are better than life:
the death of a salmon, the death of a fat pig, the death of a robber.

Art Based On: Bronze Boar, La Tène Culture. Neuvy-en-Sullias, Loiret, France. 50 BC--50 AD. Courtesy, the British Museum, London UK. Pictish Carving, St Blane's Chapel, near Kingarth, Ireland.

Illustration 8

Triad 105

Trí bí focherdat marbdili:
oss foceird a congna, fid foceird a duille, cethra focerdat a mbrénfhinda.

Three live ones that put away dead things:
a deer shedding its horn, a wood shedding its leaves, cattle shedding their coat.

Art Based On: Pictish stag, Dunfallandy stone, Scotland.

Illustration 9

Triad 72

Trí búada trebairi:
tarcud do degmnái, fognam do degfhlaith,
cóemchlód fri dagfherenn.

Three excellent things for a householder:
proposing to a good woman, serving a good
chief, exchanging for good land.

Triad 86

Trí óible adannat seirc:
gnúis, alaig, erlabra.

Three sparks that kindle love:
a face, demeanour, speech.

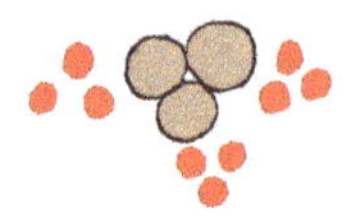

Art Based On: Gold coin of the Parisii tribe of ancient Gaul, BC. Courtesy &
currently located at the Cabinet des Médailles, France. Knotwork, bronze
mirror. Courtesy, the Liverpool Museum, Liverpool UK.

Illustration 10

Triad 146

Trí fúammann móaigthe:
fúam bó mblecht, fúam cerdchae, fúam
arathair.

Three sounds of increase:
the lowing of a cow in milk, the din of a smithy,
the swish of a plough.

Trí aithgine in domuin:
brú mná, uth bó, ness gobann.

Three renovators of the world:
the womb of a woman, a cow's udder, a smith's moulding-block.

Art Based On: Celtic Bird Brooch, Chessell Down. c. 500 A.D. Courtesy, the British Museum.

Illustration 11

Triad 225

Trí fáilti coirmthige:
immed 7 dúthracht 7 elathó.

Three welcomes of an alehouse:
plenty and kindliness and art.

Triad 205

Trí heochracha aroslicet imráitiu:
mescca, tairisiu, serc.

Three keys that unlock thoughts: drunkenness, trustfulness, love.

Art Based On: Pottery Jug, Museum number O...233, Courtesy of the British Museum. Bowl, Ceramic Fenno-Baltic Provenance Grave find, Ullna, Östra Ryd, Uppland, Sweden.

Knotwork, *Book of Kells*.

Illustration 12

Triad 99

Trí gretha tige degláich:
grith fodla, grith suide, grith coméirge.

Three shouts of a good warrior's house:
the shout of distribution, the shout of sitting down,
the shout of rising up.

Triad 80

Tréde ara carthar escara:
máin, cruth, innraccus.

Three things for which an enemy is loved:
wealth, beauty, worth.

Art Based On:

The Battersea shield. Iron Age, c. 350–50 BC. Found in the River Thames, London. Iron spearhead, c. 200-50 BC. From the River Thames. Courtesy of the British Museum, London UK.

Illustration 13

Triad 68

Trí bróin ata ferr fáilti:
brón treóit oc ithe messa, brón guirt apaig, brón feda fo mess.

Three sorrows that are better than joy:
the heaviness of a herd feeding on mast,
the heaviness of a ripe field, the heaviness
of a wood under mast.

Triad 93

Trí húathaid ata ferr sochaidi: úathad dagbríathar, úathad bó hi feór, úathad carat im chuirm.

Three fewnesses that are better than plenty: a fewness of fine words, a fewness of cows in grass, a fewness of friends around ale.*

Art Based On: Taplow Horn, 6th Century, Courtesy of the British Museum, London UK. Knotwork: the Lichfield Gospels.

Illustration 14

Triad 72

Tréde faillsigedar cach ndrochfheras: serba, miscais, midlachas.

Three unfortunate things for a householder: proposing to a bad woman, serving a bad chief, exchanging for bad land.

Triad 197

Trí dotcaid threbairi: tarcud do drochmnái, fognam do drochfhlaith, cóemchlód fri drochfherann.

Three things that show a bad man: bitterness, hatred, cowardice.

Art Based On: Sheela Na Gig, 12th Century, Cavan County Museum, Co. Cavan, Ireland. The Jelling Stone, 10th Century. Jelling, Denmark.

Illustration 15

Triad 69

Trí fáilti ata messu brón:
fáilti fir íar ndiupairt, fáilti fir íar luga
eithig, fáilti fir íar fingail.

Three rejoicings that are worse than sorrow: the joy of a man who has defrauded another, the joy of a man who has perjured himself, the joy of a man who has committed parricide.

Triad 81

Tréde ara miscnigther cara:
fogal, dognas, dímainche.

Three things for which a friend is hated: trespassing, keeping aloof, fecklessness.

Art Based On: Gold coin of the Parisii tribe of ancient Gaul, BC. Courtesy and currently located at the Cabinet des Médailles, France. Celtic sword with anthropomorphic hilt from Saint-André-de-Lidon (Charente-Maritime) France (2/1 c. BC) Knotwork: *Book of Kells*.

Illustration 16

Triad 115

Trí hairig na dúalche:
sant, cráes, étrad.

The three chief sins:
avarice, gluttony, lust.

Art Based On: The Jelling Stone, c. 900 A.D. Jelling, Denmark.

Illustration 17

Triad 95

Trí cuitbidi in domain:
fer lonn, fer étaid, fer díbech.

Three laughing-stocks of the world:
an angry man, a jealous man, a niggard.

Triad 82

Trí buirb in betha:
óc contibi sen, slán contibi galarach, gáeth
contibi báeth.

Three rude ones of the world:
a youngster mocking an old man, a healthy
person mocking an invalid, a wise man mocking
a fool.

Art Based On: Mšecké Žehrovice Head, c. 450-50 B.C., Prague National
Museum. Long Man of Wilmington. Sussex, UK. Knotwork, *Book of Kells*.

Illustration 18

Triad 116

Tréde neimthigedar crossán:
rige óile, rige théighe, rige bronn.

Three things that constitute a buffoon:
blowing out his cheek, blowing out his satchel,
blowing out his belly.

Art Based On: Mšecké Žehrovi   c. 450-50 B.C., Prague National
Museum. 17th Century Bron   n Tripod Cauldron with Initial,
auctioned SothebyUs The Oak   ...try Sale 25 April 2007. Carved
wooden scoop recovered Nunalleq, Russia, c. 1500 A.D. Knotwork, *Book
of Kells*.

Illustration 19

Triad 98

Trí fuiric thige drochduni:
debuid ar do chinn, athchosan frit, a chú
dot gabáil.

Three preparations of a bad man's house:
strife before you, complaining to you, his hound
taking hold of you.

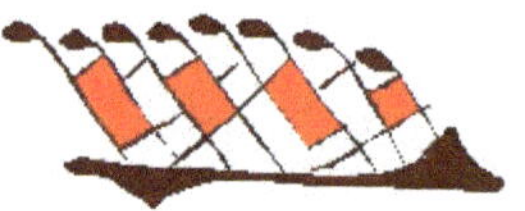

Art Based On: Zoomorphic iron figurine,Islandbridge, c. 900 A.D.Courtesy
National Museum of Ireland. Knotwork, *Book of Durrow.*

Illustration 20

Triad 67

Trí fáilti co n-íarduibi:
fer tochmairc, fer gaite, fer aisnéise.

Three rejoicings followed by sorrow:
a wooer's, a thief's, a tale-bearer's.

Triad 109

Trí hingena berta miscais do míthocod:
labra, lesca, anidna.

Three maidens that bring hatred upon
misfortune:
talking, laziness, insincerity.

Art Based On: Carved Scoop, Irish Agricultural Museum Co. Wexford,
Ireland. Knotwork, Manuscript. Bodl. 764, f. 051r, c. 1200.Bodleian Library,
Oxford, UK.

Illustration 21

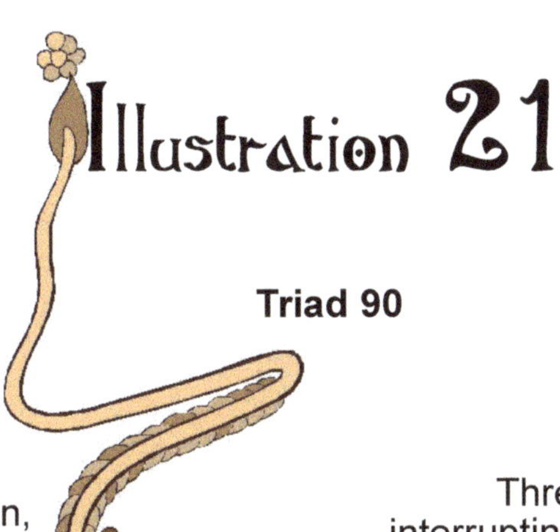

Triad 90

Trí comartha clúanaigi:
búaidriud scél, cluiche tenn,
abucht
con-imdergad.

Three ungentlemanly things:
interrupting stories, a mischievous game,
jesting so as to raise a blush.

Triad 252

Cetheora aipgitre báise:
báithe, condailbe, imresan, doingthe.

Four elements* of folly:
silliness, bias, wrangling, foulmouthedness.
* Literally, 'alphabets'.

Art Based On:
The Glauberg Prince, Glauberg Museum, Hesse, Germany. Knotwork:
Book of Ballymote.

Illustration 22

Triad 233

Trí as mó menma bís
.i. scolóc iar légad a shalm 7 gilla íar
lécud a erraid úad 7 ingen íar ndénam
mná dí.

Three whose spirits are highest:
a young scholar after having read his
psalms, a youngster who has put on
man's attire,* a maiden who has been
made a woman.
* Literally, 'who has doffed his (boy's)
clothes.

Art Based On: Ulster Maypole. Knotwork: modern decorative style.

Illustration 23

Triad 201

Trí caindle forosnat cach ndorcha:
fír, aicned, ecna.

Three candles that illumine every darkness:
truth, nature, knowledge.

Art Based On: La Tène period bronze bowl, c. 500/300 B.C. Auctioned Catawiki US, lot reference 1576931. December 2018. Knotwork: The Lindisfarne Gospels

Illustration 24

Triad 192

Trí airdi gáisse:
ainmne, faiscsiu, fáthaige.

Three signs of wisdom: patience, closeness, the gift of prophecy.

Triad 246

Trí muime ordain:
delb cháin, cuimne maith, creisine.

Three nurses of dignity:
a fine figure, a good memory, piety.

Art Based On: Small figurine, Tissø. c. 900 A.D. Courtesy the National Museum of Denmark, Copenhagen. Knotwork, *Book of Durrow*

Illustration 25

Triad 178

Trí cumtaig gáisse:
immed n-eolais, lín fássach, dagaigni do airbirt.

Three ornaments of wisdom:
an abundance of knowledge, a number of precedents, to employ a good counsel.

Triad 208

Trí seithir sognáise:
feidle, soithnges, cuinnmíne.

Three well-bred sisters:
constancy, well-spokenness, kindliness.

Art Based On: Ring Brooch, Ballinderry Crannog, cc 800 A.D. Accession number 54.2342. Courtesy Walters Art Museum, Maryland, US. Knotwork: Shandwick Stone, Easter Ross, Scotland UK.

Illustration 26

Triad 245

Trí adcoillet gáis:
anfis, doas, díchuimne.

Three things that ruin wisdom:
ignorance, inaccurate knowledge, forgetfulness.

Art Based On: Penannular Brooch, Museum number AF.2695, Courtesy of the British Museum, London UK. Knotwork: Lindisfarne Gospels

Illustration 27

Triad 118

Tréde nemthigedar sáer:
dlúthud cen fomus, cen fescred, lúd lúadrinna, béimm fo chommus.

Three things that constitute a carpenter: joining together without calculating (?), without warping (?); agility with the compass; a well-measured stroke.

Art Based On: Sarcophagus, Govan Old Church, Glasgow Scotland UK.

Illustration 28

Triad 119

Tréde neimthigedar liaig:
dígallrae, díainme, comchissi cen ainchiss.

Three things that constitute a physician: a complete cure, leaving no blemish behind, a painless examination.

Art Based On: Tully Lough Cross, National Museum of Ireland, Dublin Ireland.

Illustration 29

Triad 122

Tréde neimthigedar cruitire:
golltraige, gentraige, súantraige.

Three things that constitute a harper:
a tune to make you cry, a tune to make you
laugh, a tune to put you to sleep.

Art Based On: Brian Boru harp, Trinity College, Dublin, Ireland UK.
Knotwork: *Book of Kells*

Illustration 30

Triad 123

Tréde neimthigedar filid:
immas forosna, teinm laeda, dichetal di
chennaib.

Three things that constitute a poet:
'knowledge that illumines,' 'teinm laeda,'*
improvisation.* The names of various kinds of
incantations.
See Cormac's Glossary and Ancient Laws, s.v.

Art Based On: The Lindisfarne Gospels.

Illustration 31

Triad 177

Trí búada insci:
fosta, gáis, gairde.

Three glories of speech:
steadiness, wisdom, brevity.

Triad 179

Trí miscena indsci:
rigne, dlúithe, dulbaire.

Three hateful things in speech:
stiffness, obscurity, a bad delivery.

Art Based On: Bronze horse rider figure, c. 2nd-1st century BC. Found
near the Danube River. Ancient Resource Auction House #AC2059.
Knotwork: the Echternach Gospels.

Illustration 32

Triad 161

Trí nát fuigletar cia beith ar a ngáes:
fer adgair 7 adgairther 7 focrenar fri breith.

Three who do not adjudicate though they are
possessed of wisdom:
a man who sues, a
man who is being sued, a man who is bribed to
give judgment.

Art Based On: Bronze Harness Mount, c. 100 B.C.-100 A.D.
Anonymous sale; Bonhams, London, 6 October 2010, lot 198.

Illustration 33

Triad 173

Trí doruis gúa:
tacra fergach, fotha n-utmall n-eolais, aisnéis
cen chuimni.

Three doors of falsehood:
an angry pleading, a shifting foundation of
knowledge, giving information without
memory.

Triad 174

Trí doruis a n-aichnither fír:
frecra n-ainmnetach, ái fossad, sóud fri
fíadnu.

Three doors through which truth is recognized:
a patient answer, a firm pleading, appealing to
witnesses.

Art Based On: Gavrinis Cairn, Morbihan, Brittany. Knotwork:
Sarcophagus, Govan Old Church, Glasgow Scotland UK.

Illustration 34

Triad 194

Tréde immifoilnge gáis do báeth:
ecna, fosta, sochoisce.

Three things that make a fool wise:
learning, steadiness, docility.

Triad 195

Tréde immifoilnge báis do gáeth:
fúasnad, ferg, mesca.

Three things that make a wise man foolish:
quarreling, anger, drunkenness.

Art Based On: long spouted bronze pitcher c.500 B.C.Kleinaspergle,
Baden-Württemberg, Germany. Knotwork: *Book of Kells*.

Illustration 35

Triad 111

Trí túa ata ferr labra:
túa fri forcital, túa fri hairfitiud, túa fri procept.

Three silences that are better than speech:
silence during instruction, silence during music,
silence during preaching.

Triad 112

Three speeches that are better than silence:
inciting a king to battle, spreading knowledge
(?),* praise after reward.**

Trí labra ata ferr túa:
ochán ríg do chath, sreth immais, molad iar úag.

* 'Sreth immais,' which I have tentatively
translated by 'spreading knowledge,'

Art Based On: modern work inspired by the story of the Hazel Pool and pictish
carvings.

Illustration 36

Triad 193

Trí airdi drúisse:
bág, imresain, condailbe.

Three signs of folly:
contention, wrangling, attachment
(to everybody, to all opinions).

Art Based On: Silver early penny, Series N, c. 715-25. CM.1863-2007, De Wit
Collection. Courtesy, the Fitzwilliam Museum, Cambridge UK. Knotwork: The
Jelling Stone, c. 900 A.D. Jelling, Denmark.

Illustration 37

Triad 251

Cetheora aipgitre gáise:
ainmne, somnathe,
sobraid[e], sothnges; ar is gáeth cach
ainmnetach 7 sái cach somnath, fairsing cach
sobraid,
sochoisc cach sothengtha.

Four elements* of wisdom: patience, docility, sobriety, well-spokenness; for every patient person is wise, and every docile person is a sage, every sober person is generous, every well-spoken person is tractable.

Art Based On: Medieval Enamel Brooch, courtesy The Celtic & Prehistoric Museum, Slea Head, DIngle, Ireland. Knotwork: Pictish Cross Slab, courtesy Meigle Sculptured Stone Museum, Meigle, Perthshire, UK.

Illustration 38

Triad 200

Trí all frisa timargar béscna:
mainister, flaith, fine.

Three rocks to which lawful behaviour is tied:
a monastery, a chieftain, the family.

Art Based On: entrance stone, Newgrange, Co. Meath, Ireland.
Knotwork: Carved stone ball, Towie, Aberdeenshire, 3200–2500 BC. Courtesy the National Museum of Scotland, Edinburgh UK.

Illustration 39

Triad 202

Tréde neimthigedar ríg:
fonaidm ruirech, feis Temrach, roimse inna fhlaith.

Three things that constitute a king:
a contract with (other) kings, the feast of Tara, abundance during his reign.

Art Based On: Bronze cow and calf vessel from tomb 671, Hallstatt Archaeological Site, Austria. Courtesy Naturhistorisches Museum, Vienna, Austria.Knotwork: the Lichfield Gospels.

Illustration 40

Triad 242

Trí ata ferr do fhlaith:
fír, síth, slóg.

Three things that are best for a chief: justice, peace, an army.

Art Based On: Parade helmet, Gaul, c. 300 AD. Courtesy Historic Museum of Bern, Switzerland. Knotwork: the Lindisfarne Gospels.

Illustration 41

Triad 243

Trí ata mesa do fhlaith:
lén, brath, míairl.

Three things that are worst for a chief:
sloth, treachery, evil counsel.

Art Based On: Germanic socketed spearhead, c. 200 BC. Auction lot reference 10649425, Catawiki US. Knotwork: the Lindisfarne Gospels.

Illustration 42

Triad 189

Trí thúarascbait cach n-ainmnetach:
sámtha, túa, imdercad.

Three things that characterise every patient person:
repose, silence, blushing.

Triad 199

Trí slabrada hi cumregar clóine:
cotach, ríagail, rechtge.

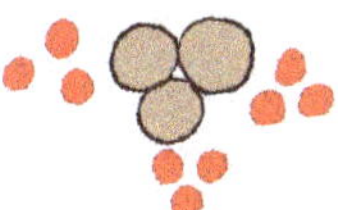

Three chains by which evil propensity is bound:
a covenant, a (monastic) rule, law.

Art Based On: Sutton Hoo purse lid, 300–1100 C.E., courtesy the Sir Paul and Lady Ruddock Gallery, London UK. Knotwork: *Book of Durrow*

Illustrations 43 + 44

I've chosen to break one long and awkward triad into two seperate pieces. Here is the original:

Triad 248

Cetheora miscne flatha:
.i. fer báeth utmall, fer dóer dímáin, fer gúach esindraic, fer labor dísceoil; ar ní tabair labrai acht do chethrur: .i. fer cerda fri háir 7 molad, fer coimgni cuimnech fri haisnéis 7 scélugud, brethem fri bretha, sencha fri senchas.

Four hatreds of a chief: a silly flighty man, a slavish useless man, a lying dishonourable man, a talkative man who has no story to tell.* For a chief does not grant speech save to four: a poet for satire and praise, a chronicler of good memory for narration and story-telling, a judge for giving judgments, an historian for ancient lore.**

Art Based On: the Book of Durrow, Illustration 41. Runic stone, Uppsala, Sweden, Illustration 42.

Illustration 45

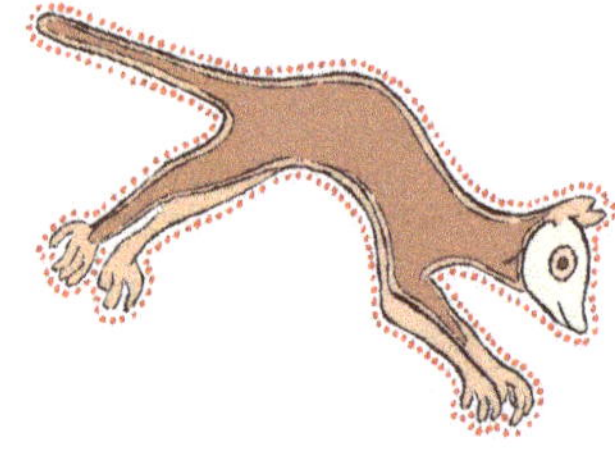

Triad 240

Trí maic beres genas do gáis: gal, gart, gaire.

Three sons whom chastity bears to wisdom: valour, generosity, laughter (filial piety?).

Art Based On: Eastern Sigillata, University of Michigan. Knotwork: *Book of Durrow*.

Illustration 46

Triad 96

Trí cuil túaithe:
flaith brécach, breithem gúach, sacart colach.

Three ruins of a tribe: a lying chief, a false judge, a lustful* priest.

Art Based On: Viking Axe, c. 800. Courtesy, Trinity College, Dublin, Ireland.
Knotwork: Runic stone, Uppsala, Sweden.

Illustration 47

This triad was recorded in Latin only, in the Yellow Book of Lecan. Meyer believed it may have been a fragment from the Counsels of Cormac. Art Based On: Poulnabrone Dolmen, the Burren, Ireland. Knotwork: The Mullamast Stone, National Museum of Archaeology, Dublin, Ireland.

About the Author

Olivia Wylie is a professional landscaper who specializes in the restoration of neglected gardens. When the weather keeps her indoors, she enjoys researching and writing about the folklore she loves and the ways it shapes human thought. She lives in Colorado with a very patient husband and a rather impatient cat. Her works can be viewed at www.leafingoutgardening.com

www.ingramcontent.com/pod-product-compliance
Lightning Source LLC
Chambersburg PA
CBHW040726010826
48981CB00030B/204